To my family, first and always—J. O'C.

For Jack and Madeleine—G. H.

The author and publisher gratefully acknowledge the assistance of John P. Riley, Director of Education & Scholarship Programs, White House Historical Association.

HOMES

EXCLUSIVE!

ADORABLE!

GREAT VIEWS!

LOCATION, LOCATION

GORGEOUS!!

EXECUTIVE HOME

WALK TO SCHOOL

LOVELY DUPLEX

WOW!

RUSTIC L

BE

1600 PENNSYLVANIA AVENUE

Beautiful 200-year-old mansion on 18 acres of land right in the heart of downtown Washington, D.C.

132 rooms with 147 windows and 28 fireplaces, including 3 kitchens, a dining room that seats more than 100 people, 32 bathrooms, 3 elevators, a tennis court, movie theater, bowling alley, outdoor swimming pool, basketball court, putting green, and separate office wings.

This dream house comes completely furnished with priceless antiques and paintings, as well as a staff of 100 people, and can be yours—absolutely free!—if you become president of the United States.

If you would like to know more about this special property, go to www.whitehouse.gov.

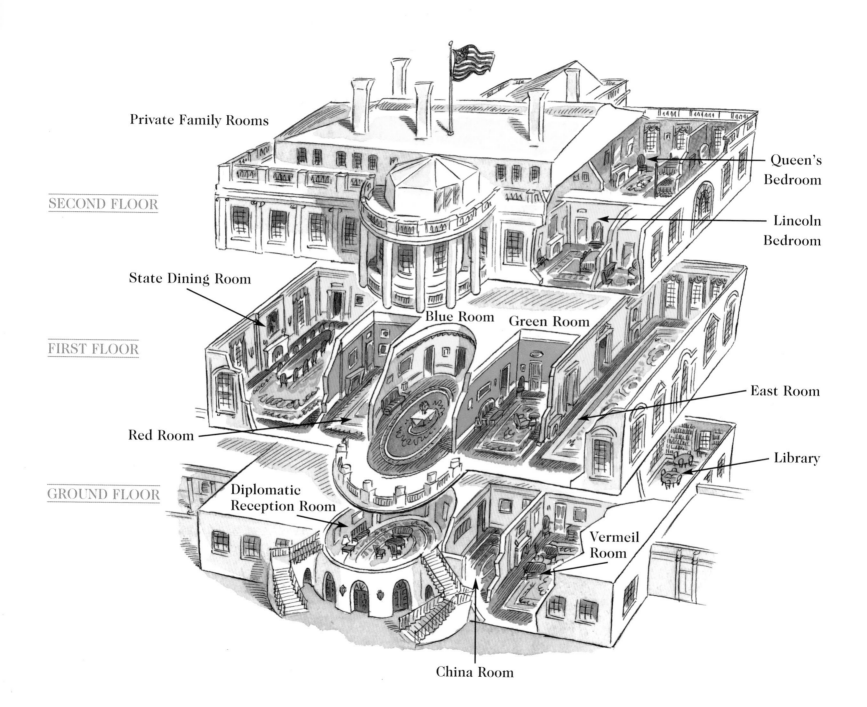

Private Family Rooms

Queen's
Bedroom

SECOND FLOOR

Lincoln
Bedroom

State Dining Room

Blue Room   Green Room

FIRST FLOOR

East Room

Red Room

Library

GROUND FLOOR

Diplomatic
Reception Room

Vermeil
Room

China Room

IF THE WALLS COULD TALK

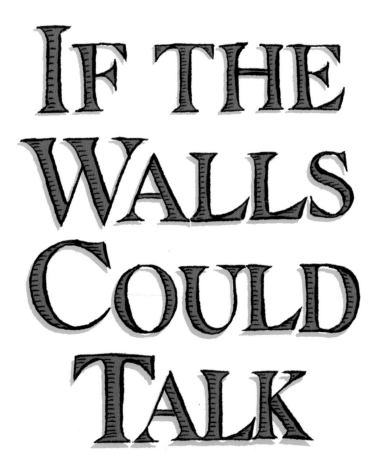

Family Life at the White House

by Jane O'Connor

★

illustrated by Gary Hovland

A Paula Wiseman Book

SIMON & SCHUSTER BOOKS FOR YOUNG READERS
New York ★ London ★ Toronto ★ Sydney

James Hoban, architect of the White House

It was **George Washington** ❶ who chose the design of the White House. He also chose the location of the capital, the heart of the new nation and home of the new Congress. He wanted the capital to be near Mount Vernon, his home in Virginia, and so it was. He was embarrassed that it was named "Washington"; he preferred "Federal City," although it wasn't much of a city yet. There were only 3,000 people, 2 unpaved streets, and no trees, and most of the houses were little more than wooden shacks.

Washington expected the president's house to grow bigger over time, and it has. Construction began in 1792, with African Americans—slaves as well as freemen—providing most of the labor. Because often there wasn't enough money for supplies or workmen, the house was still not finished when George Washington died in 1799. However, he did live to see the building begin to rise. And the outside looks very much the same today as it did in Washington's time.

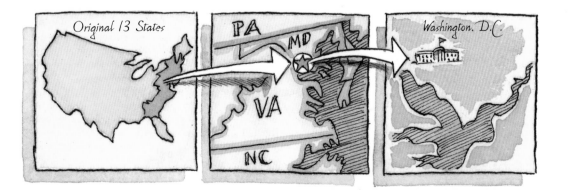

Original 13 States

PA

MD

VA

NC

Washington, D.C.

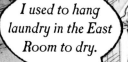

I used to hang laundry in the East Room to dry.

May none but honest and wise men rule under this roof. —John Adams

The walls were not even plastered yet.

The first tenants, **John Adams** ❷ and his wife, Abigail, moved into the house in 1800. The roof leaked; most windows had no glass; and planks led to the front door. Piles of stone and wood lay stacked in the backyard; there was also an outhouse that could accommodate three people. The Adamses lived in the White House for only four months before Thomas Jefferson became the next president.

It's big enough for two emperors, one Pope, and the Grand Lama.

attributed to
—Thomas Jefferson

I'm Tom's pet mockingbird.

I'm his grandson James, the first baby born in the White House.

People were shocked when I'd come to the door in my bathrobe and slippers.

To Do: Buy Louisiana Territory

Thomas Jefferson ❸ never liked the house very much, perhaps in part because his own design for the mansion, submitted under fake initials, hadn't been picked. While he was president, Jefferson added a long terrace with beautiful columns on either side of the house. His wife had died long before he was elected president, so his daughters and their families often came for long visits.

Well, just when the White House was finished and looking beautiful, it burned down. During the War of 1812, when **James Madison 4** was president, British troops stormed into Washington. On August 23, 1814, soldiers set fire to the White House, although not until they had finished eating the food that Dolley Madison had set out for dinner. (They also changed into clean underwear that they had found.)

Poor me! James was with the troops. I saved the portrait of George Washington, historic papers, and my parrot.

After the fire only the blackened outer walls of the house remained. The Madisons never lived in the White House again. It took two years to rebuild the mansion. In the fall of 1817, **James Monroe 5**, now president, was able to move back in, even though not all of the work was finished. He and his wife, Elizabeth, bought beautiful furniture from France; some of it is still in the Blue Room.

Our daughter, Maria, was the first child of a president to be married in the White House.

I loved to garden. I planted many trees on the south lawn.

MAPLE

BIRCH

ELM

In the 1800s presidents weren't guarded the way they are today, and the grounds of the White House were open to the public. During **John Quincy Adams**'s ❻ presidency, people might have caught a glimpse of the president—a son of John Adams—while he was gardening.

Andrew Jackson ❼ believed that anybody should be able to walk right into the White House and meet the president. At the open-house celebration on the night Jackson took office, 20,000 people showed up! Just too many! They tramped in mud, ruined rugs, broke furniture, cut bits of curtains for souvenirs, and smashed china.

So far 41 presidents have lived in the White House. Some didn't live there long; some were glad to leave; some are names rarely mentioned except in history books. But every president and his family have left their mark on the White House.

Out it goes!

I had the shortest term of any president.

I had 15 children, more than any other president.

CLICK!

Martin Van Buren ❽ auctioned off furniture that he thought was ugly. This was often the fate of unwanted White House furnishings; old china was sometimes just thrown into the Potomac River!

William Henry Harrison ❾ hardly had time to unpack. He died from pneumonia 30 days after becoming president. His wife was still at home in Ohio; she never got to live in the White House.

When **John Tyler** ❿ was president, newspapers called the White House the "Public Shabby House." But Congress wouldn't provide any money to fix it up.

During **James Polk**'s ⓫ presidency, gas lamps replaced candles and oil lamps in the White House. He was the first president to have his picture taken in the White House.

That is not my house. It's the people's house. —Franklin Pierce

Stop that!

My wife, Abigail, started the first library in the White House.

PLUK

Franklin Pierce ⓮ came to the White House in mourning over the recent death of his third and only surviving son, Bennie. His wife, Jane, had black bunting draped in the State Rooms.

Zachary Taylor ⓬ let his favorite horse, Old Whitey, graze on the White House lawn. People would pluck hairs from the horse's tail for souvenirs.

Millard Fillmore ⓭ wanted to modernize the White House. He had a bigger furnace installed and a gas stove put in the kitchen—but nobody knew how to use it.

If you are as happy, my dear sir, on entering this house as I am leaving it and going home, then you are the happiest man on earth. —James Buchanan

I loved flowers and built a greenhouse at the White House.

It's no wonder **James Buchanan** 15 was happy when his presidency was over. The country was heading toward the Civil War. Buchanan is the only president who never married. People sent all sorts of pets to the White House to keep him company.

After war broke out, sometimes Union troops camped out in the East Room. **Abraham Lincoln** 16 scolded his wife, Mary, for buying more and more expensive furniture when soldiers on the battlefield went without blankets.

It's a diversion, and we need a diversion at the White House. —Abraham Lincoln

Lincoln's words explain why he enjoyed the pranks of his spirited (some said spoiled) younger sons, Tad and Willie. Lincoln bought them two pet goats that were allowed upstairs in the bedrooms. He loved reading to his boys and roughhousing with them. It must have helped Lincoln to forget the problems facing him as president.

1865–1881

At Abraham Lincoln's funeral, souvenir hunters cut off pieces of the curtains, stole silverware, and spit tobacco juice on the rugs. The White House was in disrepair, and there were rats all over the place.

Andrew Johnson 🗓 had the house cleaned and wanted to fix up the place. But Congress wouldn't give him the money to do so. Rather than remove the rats, Congress tried to remove Johnson from office. He remained, though . . . and so did the rats.

Chester Arthur **21** never cared for the White House. He wanted it torn down and a new house built from scratch. (Here's what Congress said: No!) So, instead, Arthur had 24 wagonloads of stuff carted off and sold. Then he hired the famous designer Louis C. Tiffany to redecorate the house from top to bottom. Chester Arthur liked to give big parties . . . one was for 5,000 people!

Sometimes I wake at night in the White House and rub my eyes and wonder if it is not all a dream. —Grover Cleveland

I called her "Frank."

I called him "Uncle Cleve" because he was so much older than me.

He's 49, you know.

And she's only 21.

CLAP CLAP CLAP

CLAP CLAP CLAP

CLAP CLAP CLAP CLAP

Grover Cleveland 22 was married in the Blue Room at the White House. When he lost the next election, his beautiful and popular wife, Frances, told the staff that they'd be back in four years. And she was right. Cleveland is the only president whose second term didn't come right after his first.

By the end of the 1800s the White House was starting to burst at the seams. The president's staff, which kept growing larger, still worked in offices on the second floor. The president's family didn't have enough room or privacy. **Benjamin Harrison** 23—grandson of William Henry Harrison—and his wife, Caroline, came with their daughters and grandchildren. The Harrisons put up the first Christmas tree inside the White House. Now each year the ornaments have a theme, such as state flowers, Mother Goose characters, or birds of America.

I had electric lights installed.

But we didn't like to touch the switches because of shocks.

After **William McKinley** 25, who was kindhearted, cheerful, and one of the most popular presidents ever, was shot and killed, the Secret Service assigned agents to protect the president and his family.

My wife, Ida, didn't like the color yellow. She banned it from the White House.

During **Grover Cleveland**'s 24 second term the Clevelands' daughter Esther was born in the White House. So far she is the only child of a president who has been born there.

I don't think any family has enjoyed the White House more than we have.

—Theodore Roosevelt

I made "White House" the official name of the mansion.

V ice President **Teddy Roosevelt** 26 became president after William McKinley died. He was only 42 years old, and right away he loved being president. What energy he had! After a new tennis court was installed, the president is said to have played 91 games in one day. The six rambunctious Roosevelt kids liked to sled down the stairs on cookie trays, walk on stilts through the hallways, roller-skate in the East Room, and shimmy up the flagpole.

The White House was now 100 years old. Edith, Teddy Roosevelt's calm, dependable wife, oversaw a major renovation. There wasn't enough office space, so the greenhouses were torn down and a new wing was built—the West Wing, where the president's Oval Office is located.

I'm glad to be going. This is the lonesomest place on earth. —William Howard Taft

I was the first president with a car. I turned the stables into a garage.

Unlike Roosevelt, **William Taft 27** didn't enjoy being president, but at least he could relax in a hot bath after a special tub was made for him. Taft was a *big* guy—6 feet 2 inches tall and more than 300 pounds. His tub could fit four ordinary-size men.

Suddenly we became goldfish in a bowl.
—Eleanor Wilson McAdoo, Woodrow Wilson's daughter

I think you missed a spot.

During the 19th century the White House vegetable gardens, as well as cows and pigs kept on the grounds, provided food for the First Families. By **Woodrow Wilson**'s ㉘ time, however, food was bought at grocery stores and butcher shops. So, why did the Wilsons keep sheep on the lawn? In 1917 so many men were needed as soldiers to fight in World War I that the Wilsons didn't think it was right to have gardeners. Instead, sheep trimmed the White House grass. Knitted socks for soldiers came from their wool.

Let 'em look in if they want to. It's their house. —Florence Harding

During one of his many poker games **Warren Harding** 29 gambled away a whole set of White House china. There were many scandals while Harding was president; he liked playing golf more than working at his job. Laddie Boy, Harding's beloved Airedale, had his own servant at the White House and his own chair at cabinet meetings.

Calvin Coolidge **30** hardly ever cracked a smile. His warm and vibrant wife, Grace, was a popular First Lady, though. The Coolidges had a new roof put on and converted the attic into a floor of bedrooms and offices. **Herbert Hoover 31** was a self-made millionaire, and he didn't like dealing with servants. He never looked at or spoke to them. Servants at the White House had to duck into closets if President Hoover came down a hall.

I never forget that I live in a house owned by all the American people and that I have been given their trust. —Franklin D. Roosevelt

I was elected four times. I loved the job.

Fala, FDR's Scottie

The Roosevelts lived in the White House for 12 years, longer than any other family. Because of polio, **Franklin D. Roosevelt** ㉜, or "FDR" as he was called, was confined to a wheelchair. Schoolchildren across the country raised money to build an indoor pool at the White House so that he could exercise.

A house that is on exhibition should look its best at all times.

—Eleanor Roosevelt

I was the first First Lady to hold a press conference.

NEW DEAL FACTS & FIGURES

It was difficult for FDR to travel, so his wife, Eleanor, became his eyes and ears. She was away so much that a newspaper ran a fake headline: MRS. ROOSEVELT SPENDS NIGHT IN WHITE HOUSE. Eleanor was different from First Ladies before her. She had a career—many, in fact. She taught school, wrote a daily newspaper column and a best-selling book, and always told the president exactly what she thought he should do. She was too busy to spend much time furnishing and redecorating the White House. But in 1942 the East Wing was expanded. It houses a movie theater and offices.

It's a glamorous prison. —Harry S. Truman

After one of the legs on his daughter's piano broke through the second floor, **Harry S. Truman** 33 had the White House inspected. Good thing he did. A building engineer told him that the house was "standing up purely from habit." In 1948 President Truman, his wife, Bess, and their daughter, Margaret, moved out while the inside of the house was gutted and rebuilt.

We moved back four years later.

33

World War II General **Dwight Eisenhower** ③④ and his wife, Mamie, moved into a new and improved White House. "Ike" and Mamie often ate dinner on trays while they watched television. They had his 'n' hers sets because they liked different shows.

Not since Teddy Roosevelt had there been a family with young children living in the White House. And what a family! President **John F. Kennedy** 35 and his wife, Jacqueline, seemed like glamorous movie stars. The nation loved watching the antics of their daughter, Caroline, and her little brother, "John-John." The Kennedys took great pride in the White House. If the lawn looked dry when important guests were coming, Kennedy would have it spray-painted green.

Jacqueline Kennedy is remembered for turning the White House into a place of culture and beauty, restoring rooms with furniture and belongings of past First Families. In 1962 Jackie gave a television tour of the White House. Forty-two million people watched. Now the White House is the number-one tourist attraction in Washington, D.C.

Only hours after John F. Kennedy was shot and killed in Dallas, Texas, **Lyndon Johnson** 36 was sworn in to office. For Johnson, the unpopular war in Vietnam hung over his years in the White House like a dark cloud. Antiwar protesters would often demonstrate across the street.

STOP THE KILLING

HANDS OFF VIETNAM

WAR IS NOT ANSW

There's a wall around me that no one gets through.

STOP THE WAR

SEND OUR TROOPS OME

GET OUT OF NAM

MAKE LOVE NOT WAR

36

When I walked through the rooms of the White House, I had a constant sense of a host of companions . . . I knew that I walked with history. —Lady Bird Johnson

Picture a giant fish bowl with spotlights . . .
—Julie Nixon Eisenhower, Richard Nixon's daughter

Maybe putting in the press room wasn't such a good idea.

Did you know about the Watergate break-in?

Because of political scandals, **Richard Nixon 37** is the only president to resign and move out of the White House before his term was over. While he lived there, he put in a one-lane bowling alley and covered up FDR's indoor swimming pool to make a press room for reporters.

Now more than 200 years old, the White House is where the past lives and where history is made every day. It is where the president works. It is also a museum. But each day after the public leaves, the velvet ropes are taken away and the rugs are rolled out. It becomes a home again, a home that changes with every family lucky enough to live there.

Jimmy Carter's 39 young daughter, Amy, had a tree house, where she could find peace and privacy. At times Carter probably wanted to join her there to escape from economic and foreign problems that troubled his presidency.

Gerald Ford 38 had an outdoor pool built so he could stay in shape. The Fords' youngest child, Susan, had her senior prom at the White House.

Ronald Reagan 40, who was nearly 70 when he took office, was the oldest president ever and an actor in Hollywood before he entered politics. He met his future wife, Nancy, on a movie set. They liked to give lavish parties at the White House.

George Bush **41** came from a rich and powerful New England family. His wife, Barbara, wrote a best-selling book about their dog Millie's life at the White House.

George W. Bush **43** was the son of George Bush. He and his wife, Laura, had two teenage daughters, Jenna and Barbara—the first White House twins.

We honor all the presidents who came before us and all who will come after.

Despite personal scandals and an impeachment trial, **Bill Clinton** **42** was a popular president. He liked to jog and had a running track set up on the White House grounds.

When John Adams moved into the White House, his wife, Abigail, was still in Philadelphia. He wrote her a letter, part of which has come to be known as the White House Blessing. It is carved into the mantel in the State Dining Room, pictured on the preceding page. These are the words:

"I pray Heaven to bestow the best of Blessings on this House and all that shall hereafter inhabit it. May none but honest and wise Men ever rule under this roof."

★ ★ ★ ★ ★ ★ ★ ★ ★ ★ ★ Ask the Presidents ★ ★ ★ ★ ★ ★ ★ ★ ★ ★ ★ ★ ★ ★ ★

President Washington, where did you live while you were president?

First in New York City, then in Philadelphia.

President John Adams, who owns the White House?

The people of the United States.

President Jefferson, where does the First Family live?

On the second and third floors, in rooms not open to the public.

President Madison, was the White House always white?

Yes, originally whitewash was used to protect the porous sandstone from freezing.

President Monroe, how much paint does it take to cover the outside of the house?

About 300 gallons.

President John Quincy Adams, was the president's home always called the White House?

No, at first people called it the "President's House." But by my time the name "White House" had stuck. People also still refer to it as the "Executive Mansion."

President Jackson, will people see the president if they visit the White House?

In my day they very well might have—but not now.

President Van Buren, do people send many gifts to the White House?

Yes, I was once given a wheel of cheese that weighed more than 700 pounds! Other kinds of gifts become part of the White House collection.

President William Henry Harrison, how many presidents have died inside the White House?

Two. I did, and so did Zachary Taylor.

President Tyler, how many children have lived in the White House?

It's hard to say exactly, what with presidents' children, grandchildren, and other relatives having lived there. One book estimates about 200 children have lived there.

President Polk, why is "Hail to the Chief" played to signal the entrance of the president?

It's a tradition—one that I started.

President Taylor, what is the most famous room in the White House?

Probably the East Room, where weddings and funerals have been held and important bills have been signed.

President Fillmore, how long may a president and his family live in the White House?

Only while the president is in office.

President Pierce, while in the White House, does the president have to pay rent?

No, the president's family lives in the White House rent-free.

President Buchanan, what are the State Rooms?

The formal public rooms such as the East Room and others on the first floor.

President Lincoln, did you ever sleep in the Lincoln Bedroom?

No, in my day it wasn't a bedroom—it was my office.

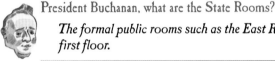
President Andrew Johnson, is the White House the biggest house in the United States?

Not anymore, but it was until about 1865.

President Grant, how many children of presidents have been married in the White House?

Nine, including my daughter, Nellie. John Adams, son of John Quincy Adams, was the only son to be married there.

President Hayes, how many people make phone calls to the White House?

Now about 5,000 calls come in each day.

President Garfield, are there elevators in the White House?

Yes, the first one was installed in 1881.

President Arthur, where did you keep all of your clothes?

In chests and standing wardrobes. The White House had no closets until the early 1900s.

President Cleveland, how many presidents have been married in the White House?

So far, just me.

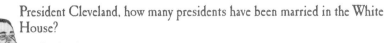
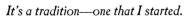

★ ★

 President Benjamin Harrison, is the First Family required to live in the White House?

No—in fact, the Clevelands sometimes lived in another home for greater privacy.

 President McKinley, do Secret Service agents guard the First Family 24/7?

Yes, but in the private rooms of the White House the family is left alone.

 President Theodore Roosevelt, are pets allowed in the White House?

Oh, yes! My children kept badgers, mice, raccoons, pigs, parrots, dogs, cats, baby bears, snakes, a one-legged rooster, and a kangaroo rat that sat on the breakfast table eating sugar.

 President Taft, how many bathrooms are in the White House?

Now there are 32. But my huge bathtub was removed, and its whereabouts is unknown.

 President Wilson, why is the White House sometimes closed to the public?

In times of war the mansion is closed to the public because of security concerns.

 President Harding, may presidents get rid of furniture and china that they don't like?

Not anymore. The White House is a museum; all of the furnishings in the public rooms belong to the house.

 President Coolidge, does each First Family bring belongings of their own when they move in?

Yes.

 President Hoover, would you say a little more about that?

Each family brings furniture and personal possessions to decorate the private rooms.

 President Franklin D. Roosevelt, which family lived in the White House the longest?

Mine! We lived there for twelve years.

President Truman, could another First Family ever live there longer?

No. Since 1951 presidents have been allowed to serve only two terms.

 President Eisenhower, is the White House the only official house of the president?

Yes, but in national parkland in Maryland there is also Camp David, a presidential retreat named after my grandson.

 President Kennedy, does the president get a salary?

Yes. Now it is almost $400,000. However, both President Hoover and I chose not to accept the salary.

 President Lyndon Johnson, are there ghosts in the White House?

President Truman said, "The place is haunted, sure as shootin'," and Lady Bird said she felt a "presence" at times, although she never saw any ghosts. Abraham Lincoln's ghost is the one people spot most often.

 President Nixon, what is the most distinctive feature of the house?

The oval rooms. There are three oval rooms in the house, as well as the Oval Office in the West Wing.

 President Ford, how big is the White House staff?

Now there is a staff of about 100 people who run the house.

 President Carter, has the house ever been repainted?

Yes, more than 40 times. During my term workers scraped away 42 old layers of paint before getting down to the original sandstone.

 President Reagan, what is the oldest object in the White House?

It's hard to say—perhaps the famous portrait of George Washington that Dolley Madison saved.

 President George Bush, are there still rats in the White House?

I don't know, but when we lived there, my wife, Barbara, saw one in the pool. It swam right past her.

 President Clinton, may a former president use Air Force One?

No, only the president who is currently in office gets to use the plane.

 President George W. Bush, is there a portrait of every president and First Lady in the White House?

No, unfortunately not every single one. The Hayeses began the tradition of putting up portraits of the presidents, and Edith Roosevelt, Teddy's wife, started a portrait gallery of First Ladies.

★ ★

BIBLIOGRAPHY

Books for Younger Readers

Davis, Kenneth C. *Don't Know Much About the Presidents.* New York: HarperCollins, 2002.

Harness, Cheryl. *Ghosts of the White House.* New York: Simon and Schuster, 1998.

Karr, Kathleen. *It Happened in the White House: Extraordinary Tales from America's Most Famous Home.* New York: Hyperion, 2000.

Mattern, David B. and Holly C. Schulman, eds. *The Selected Letters of Dolley Payne Madison.* Charlottesville: University of Virginia Press, 2003.

Remini, Robert V. *The Life of Andrew Jackson.* New York: HarperCollins, 1988.

Sandler, Martin W. *Presidents.* New York: HarperCollins, 1995.

Books for Older Readers

Bush, Barbara. *Millie's Book: As Dictated to Barbara Bush.* New York: William Morrow, 1990.

Hurd, Charles. *The White House Story.* New York: Hawthorn, 1966.

Jensen, Amy La Follette. *The White House and Its Thirty-Two Families.* New York: McGraw-Hill, 1956.

Leish, Kenneth W. *The White House.* New York: Newsweek, 1972.

Seale, William. *The President's House: A History,* Vols. 1–2. Washington, D.C.: White House Historical Association, 1986.

Whitcomb, John and Claire Whitcomb. *Real Life at the White House: 200 Years of Daily Life at America's Most Famous Residence.* New York: Routledge Press, 2000.

Wead, Doug. *All the Presidents' Children: Triumph and Tragedy in the Lives of America's First Families.* New York: Atria, 2003.

SIMON & SCHUSTER BOOKS FOR YOUNG READERS
An imprint of Simon & Schuster Children's Publishing Division
1230 Avenue of the Americas, New York, New York 10020
Text copyright © 2004 by Jane O'Connor
Illustrations copyright © 2004 by Gary Hovland
All rights reserved, including the right of reproduction in whole or in part in any form.
SIMON & SCHUSTER BOOKS FOR YOUNG READERS is a trademark of Simon & Schuster, Inc.
Book design by Greg Stadnyk
The text for this book is set in Caslon 224, Caslon Antique, and Michelangelo.
The illustrations for this book are rendered in ink and watercolor.
Manufactured in the United States of America
10 9 8 7 6 5 4 3 2 1
Library of Congress Cataloging-in-Publication Data
O'Connor, Jane.
If the walls could talk : family life at the White House / Jane O'Connor ; illustrated by Gary Hovland.—1st ed.
p. cm.
"A Paula Wiseman Book."
ISBN 0-689-86863-4
1. Presidents—United States—History—Juvenile literature. 2. Presidents—United States—Family relationships—Juvenile literature. 3. Presidents—United States—Biography—Juvenile literature. 4. White House (Washington, D.C.)—History—Juvenile literature. I. Hovland, Gary, ill. II. Title.
E176.1.O28 2004
973'.09'9—dc22
2004004832